THE INTERGALACTIC BUS TRIP

Martin Oliver

Illustrated by
Brenda Haw and Martin Newton

Designed by
Patrick Knowles and Kim Blundell

Series Editor: Gaby Waters

Contents

About this Book

The Intergalactic Bus Trip is an exciting adventure story with a difference. The difference is that you can take a part in the adventure.

Throughout the book, there are lots of tricky puzzles and perplexing problems for you to solve. You will need to find the answers to understand the next episode in the story.

Look at the pictures carefully and watch out for vital clues. Sometimes you will need to flick back through the book to help you find an answer.

There are extra clues on page 43 and you can check your answers on pages 44 to 48.

Just turn the page to begin the adventure . . .

The Computer Game

Tom and Izzy were playing a record-breaking game of 'Robot Raiders'. The score was 2,325,998 to 2,325,999 and Tom was winning. He had never got this far before. In fact, no one had ever got this far before.

Tom's spaceship dodged and weaved through a hail of missiles and exploding bombs. He took careful aim and pressed the trigger.

My score's been wiped out!

Sssh. Look at the computer.

CLICK. They were plunged into darkness and a strange humming sound filled the room. The computer buzzed and whirred.

Tom yelled at the computer, but Izzy took no notice. She was staring at the screen in surprise. It began to glow an eerie green, as a series of strange symbols appeared.

"I think it's some sort of message," said Izzy, studying the screen. "But I'm not sure how to read it."

"Forget it," said Tom, crossly. "The computer must be broken."

Can you read the message?

5

On to the Bus

A few days later, Tom and Izzy were late for the cinema. As they ran down the road, a Number Nine bus drew up beside them.

"Come on. Let's take the bus," Izzy shouted, jumping aboard.

On the magazine cover: **Planet Earth** — **Tourist Guide**

"Two tickets please," said Tom, looking at the driver in surprise.

Izzy walked on down the bus towards some empty seats at the back.

The doors slammed shut. As Izzy looked around, she spotted several very odd things ... this was not a normal bus.

How many odd things can you see?

Lift-Off

Before Izzy could say anything, there was a loud bang and the bus lurched forwards. Tom went flying as the bus moved faster and faster. It hurtled along the High Street and swerved round a corner shop.

Passengers and papers flew everywhere. Tom gazed out of the window in disbelief as the bus left the ground and soared into the air. Houses and trees disappeared below as the bus roared onwards and upwards through the clouds.

Izzy hung on to her seat and watched in amazement as Tom floated up. What was happening? Tom drifted past her and bumped gently against the window. He stared out in horror, beginning to feel very ill. Where were they going?

What they needed was a map. As Tom slumped down beside her, Izzy remembered seeing one, but where was it? She racked her brains. Just then she felt a tap on her shoulder . . .

Can you find the bus map?

Roger the Martian

A large eye blinked at Izzy. The eye was attached to a long, wobbly antenna and the antenna was connected to a smiling, green thing.

"Perhaps I can help," said the thing, pulling the bus map out of his pocket.

Izzy gawped in amazement. Who was this strange creature?

"My name is Roger," he said. "I'm on my way to Zenos, but I come from Mars."

"You speak very good English," Izzy exclaimed.

"Of course," replied the Martian. "I went to Earth on a school trip last year."

Izzy asked Roger if he knew how to get back to Earth. But Roger looked puzzled and scratched his head.

"I think you should get off at the next stop," he said, studying the map.

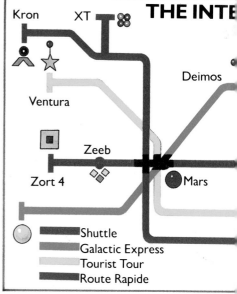

Kron   XT   **THE INTE**

Ventura   Deimos

Zeeb

Zort 4   Mars

Shuttle
Galactic Express
Tourist Tour
Route Rapide

What is the next stop?

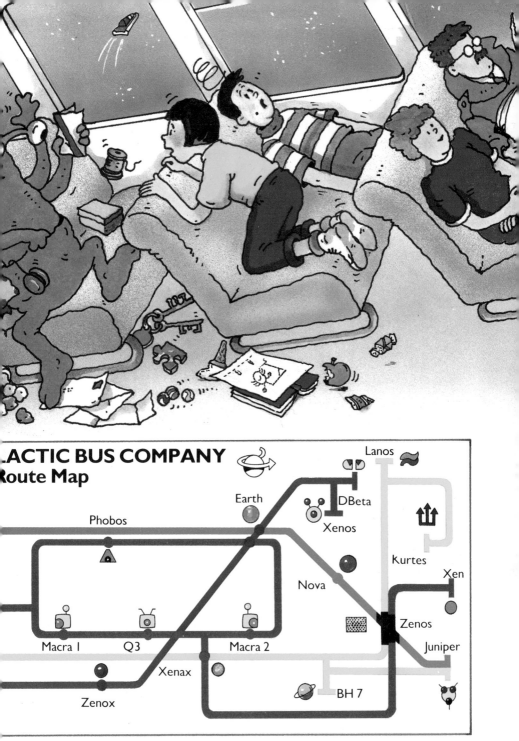

The Arrival Processing Plant

As the droid driver announced the next stop, the bus began to orbit a pink planet. It hovered over the landing zone and started its descent. Izzy wondered if she would ever see home again.

The bus bounced on to the cosmic concrete. It screeched to a halt and there was a mad scramble as all the other passengers rushed off the bus.

BLACK HAIRED BEINGS

GREEN THINGS

NON-MARTIANS

LUGGAGE

NO EXIT

WELCOME TO NOVA NEW TOWN ARRIVAL PROCESSING PLANT

"Wh... where are we?" Tom stammered, opening his eyes.

"We're on Nova," replied Roger, heading towards the door. "Follow me. My friend Norman lives here. He's bound to know how to get you on the next Earth-bound bus."

Tom and Izzy jumped off the bus and saw eleven doors ahead of them.

"We must find a door that we can all go through, or we'll lose each other," said Roger.

Which door can they go through?

In Nova New Town

Roger whisked them through the Processing Plant and out into Nova New Town. He fumbled in his voluminous pockets and pulled out a very grubby school photograph.

"There's Norman," said Roger. "He's sitting to my left, third from the right, behind the blue blob."

At the bottom, Norman had scribbled his address. Roger looked up and groaned. All the buildings looked the same to him. How would they ever find Norman?

"I know," said Izzy, suddenly. "Follow me."

Can you identify Norman? Where does he live?

Flat 3, floor 14, Megalith Tower (the flat fronted blue building with a flat roof — very close to the monorail).

Action Replay

Izzy dashed ahead. But three minutes, two left turns and one dead-end later, she noticed that Tom and Roger were no longer following.

Retracing her steps, she turned a corner and gasped. Roger was lying on the ground. He had turned a very funny shade of turquoise.

"Roger, are you O.K?" she asked. "You don't look well."

"I'm fine," groaned Roger. "Just a bit off colour. But Tom..."

Roger wasn't sure what had happened to Tom. He struggled to his feet, looking very unsteady.

"My photographic memory might help," he said. "But it's a bit confused."

Izzy watched in amazement as Roger projected a series of photographs into the air. If she could put them into order, she would be able to find out what had happened to Tom.

Can you work out what happened to Tom?

Norman the Novan

Roger and Izzy looked at each other, their minds racing. Why had the aliens snatched Tom? Where were they taking him? And who were they?

Roger directed his antennae at the pink Novan sky.

"I can see the kidnappers' ship," he shouted. "Quick. We must get back to the bus and follow them."

They set off through the streets, turned left and THUD. They collided with a small, round, bouncy creature.

18/15/7/21/5/18/15/2/15/20/19/8/9/16/20/15/2/1/19/5/
15/14/18/15/2/15/20/9/3/1/13/9/19/19/9/15/14/20/15/
11/9/4/14/1/16/5/1/18/20/8/20/8/9/14/7/19/21/3/3/5/
19/19/6/21/12/8/5/23/9/12/12/18/5/13/1/9/14/4/5/5/
16/6/18/15/26/5/14/6/15/18/g/i/13/9/3/18/15/13/9/14/
21/20/5/19/2/5/6/15/18/5/2/5/9/14/7/20/1/11/5/14/20/
15/20/8/5/3/8/1/12/12/5/14/7/5/3/8/1/13/2/5/18/1/20/
i/c/d/a/5/14/4/15/6/13/5/19/19/1/7/5

"Norman!" exclaimed Roger. "We've been looking for you. This is my new Earth-thing friend . . ."

"Yes I know. Hello Izzy," said Norman, waggling his outsize ears proudly. "I overheard. I think I can help you by zeroing in on the kidnappers' frequency."

Norman frowned. His orange hair stood on end and his ears buzzed as he relayed a long series of numbers. What did they mean? Was it some sort of coded message?

Can you decode the message? Who has kidnapped Tom and where is he being taken?

19

Back on the Bus

THE SHOOTING

STAR SNACK BAR

R oger kept one eye trained on the kidnappers' ship, as he and Izzy followed Norman back to the bus. Puffing and panting they clambered aboard.

"I'll drive," wheezed Roger, brandishing a piece of yellow plastic. "Here's my universal driving licence. Hang on tight. We'll soon get Tom back from those Rogue Robots."

The bus taxied into the take-off area. Roger pressed the power pedal and they began to accelerate. Izzy was just about to secure the doors when, to her surprise, she saw Tom running towards the bus.

"Abort take-off," shouted Roger as he spotted the advancing figure.

Izzy stared hard at Tom for a moment. All of a sudden, she hit the automatic door-locking button.

"Take off!" she yelled. "It's a trick."

Is she right?

On the Vapour Trail

Roger checked the instruments again and flicked the lift-off lever. Within seconds they were space-borne, tracking the kidnappers' route with the help of Norman's sonic ear sensors. But just as they rounded a deserted, green planet, Norman's ears went floppy.

"The signal's faded," he cried. "I've lost track of the Robots' ship."

Roger scanned the sky with his telescopic eye. All he could see was a tangled web of vapour trails around Interstellar Junction 15. Then Izzy had a brain wave.

"Let's follow the kidnappers' vapour trail," she said.

Can you follow the vapour trail?

Collision Course

The bus wove its way through the tangled trails out into open space. It whizzed through the cosmos, past satellites and stars until, at last, the Robots' ship was in sight.

Suddenly Roger saw a meteor hurtling towards the bus. He slammed on the brakes but it was too late. They were on a collision course. Izzy dived for cover...

Minutes later, she crawled out from under her seat feeling dazed. Roger was looking at the engine and Norman was rummaging in the repair kit.

"What happened?" asked Izzy, peering at the engine.

"We crash-parked on this service satellite," replied Norman. "The engine's broken."

"Then we must fix it," said Izzy, picking up a spanner.

Can you repair the engine?

The Microfilm Map

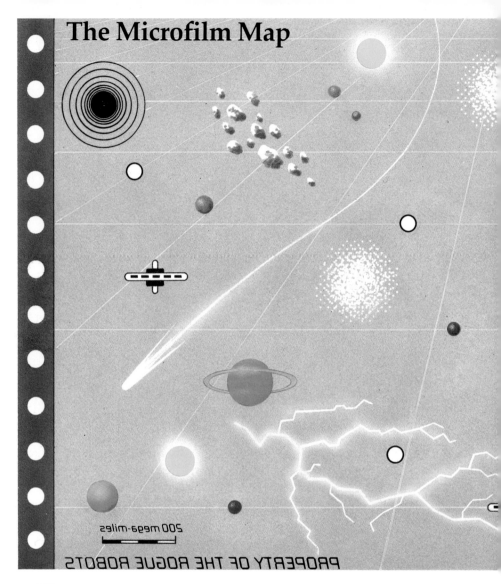

200 mega-miles

PROPERTY OF THE ROGUE ROBOTS

Roger pressed the starter switch. The engine spluttered into life and the bus roared off. Norman and Roger scanned the stratosphere with their eyes and ears open wide, but the kidnappers had vanished without trace.

"It's hopeless," snuffled Izzy. "We'll never find Tom."

Roger parked the bus on the edge of a small sun. He dug into his pockets for a handkerchief. Out fell a tiny square of microfilm.

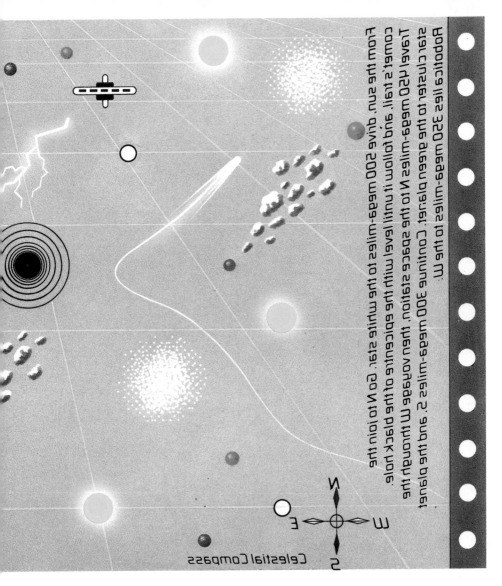

"I'd forgotten about this," he said, holding it up to the light. "I found it on the ground when Tom disappeared."

"It's a microfilm map," Izzy exclaimed. "And it belongs to the Rogue Robots."

Then she saw some strange writing on one side of the map. If only she could decipher it, she was sure it would lead them to the Robots' Planet.

Where is the bus?
What is the route to Robotica?

Speeding on the Skyway

Roger started up the bus again and set off towards Robotica. They drove on and on, through mega-mile after mega-mile of empty space until they reached the start of the South Orbital Skyway. The bus slowed down and Izzy looked at the time read-out on the Skyway Signpost in dismay.

Time was running out. The Robots would reach their base in 26 micro-minutes and the bus was a long way behind. Izzy hoped the read-out might be wrong. But it wasn't. The green dashboard clock showed the same time and the dashboard clock was never wrong. Roger hit the boost button.

Cosmic time check at 93:15. Observation bulletin to all patrols. One red bus entering South Orbital Skyway.

XR7 EXIT : 900 mega-miles
PLUTON EXIT : 855 mega-miles
MAX. SPEED 60 mega-miles per micro-minute
MAX. SPEED 55 mega-miles per micro-minute
MAX. SPEED 75 mega-miles per micro-minute

macro-hours > 93 : 15 < micro-minutes

The bus rocketed down the skyway. As they passed the Pluton exit, they saw a flashing light and screeched to a halt in front of a grim-looking skyway patrolman.

"You're booked," he growled. "You were speeding on the skyway."

Roger didn't know what to say. After all, he had been driving very fast...

"No we weren't," cried Izzy. "And I can prove it."

Was the bus speeding on the skyway?

Searching for the Base

695 mega-miles further on, the planet Robotica was in sight. The bus slowed down and Roger put the controls onto auto-orbit. He stuck his antennae out of the window and scanned the alien landscape below. There was no sign of Tom or the Robots. Where was the base?

Just then, Norman's ears began to buzz. He pointed down to the planet surface.

"I'm picking up high-frequency signals," he explained.

"Where are they coming from?" asked Izzy, excitedly.

Norman pin-pointed seven landmarks: the sapphire stone, the space-ship wreck, the tower roof, the aerial mast, the blue bridge, the ventilation shaft and the red rock.

"They make a pattern," said Izzy, drawing imaginary lines between the signals. "Perhaps they will lead us to the base."

Where is the Robots' base?

The Secret Sequence

Crash, bang, bump. Roger landed the bus. They scrambled into space suits and floated out of the door.

The planet was covered in a thick, invisible gas. Drifting was easy, but getting anywhere was much more tricky.

Roger and Norman swam ahead towards a door in the green cliff. It was locked.

Norman pointed to the panel of numbered buttons beside the door. The only way to open it was to tap in a special, secret number sequence.

A sudden gust of gas knocked over a dustbin beside the door. Roger snatched at the scraps of floating space debris. Numbers were scribbled on them.

"I think they make a sequence," said Roger, enlarging the scraps with his right eye. "We must fit them together to find out."

Some of the pieces were missing which left gaps in the sequence. But it wasn't hard to work out the missing numbers.

Izzy paddled up to the door and punched the sequence onto the numbered keys. Very slowly, the door slid open.

What are the missing numbers?

Inside the Base

Alarm Centre

Rifle Range

Slime Pit

Beyond the door, everything was dark. Izzy hoped that she was looking braver than she felt as she entered the base.

"We must be quiet," Roger whispered. "The Rogue Robots will have sound sensors hidden all over the place."

CLANG. Norman dropped his helmet. They stopped still and held their breath, waiting for an alarm to ring. But all they could hear was the helmet bouncing down some steps.

"Whoops," said Norman and scuttled after his helmet.

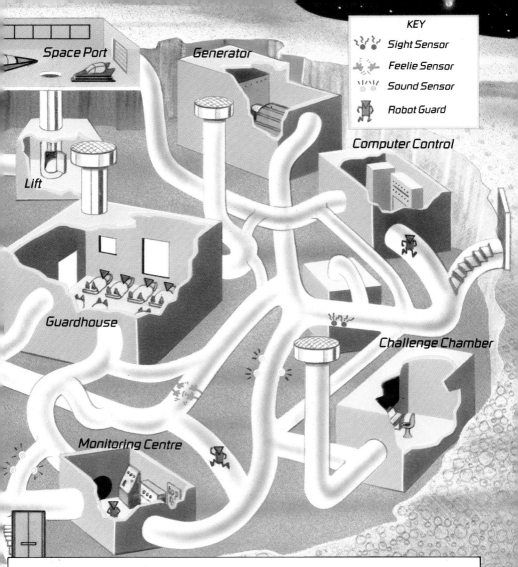

KEY

🐾 Sight Sensor

🦋 Feelie Sensor

〰️ Sound Sensor

🤖 Robot Guard

Space Port

Generator

Computer Control

Lift

Guardhouse

Challenge Chamber

Monitoring Centre

Roger and Izzy followed on tiptoes, down the steps and straight on to a junction. Here they turned left and felt a cool, gassy breeze from a ventilation shaft on their right. They followed the passage as it bent round in a U shape, ignoring the turning to the left.

The passage bent to the left and then to the right where it forked in two. In the middle of the two forks, Izzy spotted a map of the base. Now they could work out how to get to Tom.

Where are they and how can they reach Tom?

The Key to the Challenge Chamber

Ahead lay the locked door of the Challenge Chamber. Norman acted as listen-out, while Roger examined the lock.

"We need a key like this," said Roger, projecting the image of a key shape.

Izzy saw a bunch of keys hanging on the wall. One of them was bound to fit the lock. She reached up and picked them off the hook...

"No!" yelled Roger.

Too late! Sirens wailed and red lights flashed as Izzy fumbled with the keys.

"Hurry up," yelled Norman. "I can hear a troop of Robots and they're coming this way."

Which key will open the door to the Challenge Chamber?

Robot Raiders

They sprinted through the open door as the Rogue Robots started firing their stun guns. Izzy slammed the door shut and ran towards Tom. He was strapped to a chair in front of a giant 'Robot Raiders' screen.

"What are you doing playing computer games?" gasped Izzy.

"I'm not," gulped Tom. "It's for real this time. If I lose, the Robots will destroy us."

Roger and Norman looked puzzled, so Izzy explained.

"Tom has to isolate each of the enemy rockets," she said. "But he only has three defence discs left to fire."

"What's a defence disc?" asked Norman, feeling confused.

"It's a green circle, exactly like the one on the screen," Tom explained.

All of a sudden, a menacing metallic voice rang out through the chamber.

"No one can beat the Rogue Robots," snarled the voice. "You were fools to challenge us. Now you will die. There is no way out."

"That's what you think," yelled Izzy, grabbing the controls from Tom's hand.

Can you beat the computer?

Laser Maze

The lights began to flicker and the screen went blank as the metallic voice echoed through the chamber.

"You may think you've beaten us, but we shall win in the end. This planet is programmed to self-destruct and even if you leave it in time, you will never escape the laser maze.

They didn't wait to hear any more. Roger untied Tom and they all sprinted out of the chamber, back along smoke-filled corridors, out of the base and onto the bus.

Roger set the controls for vertical take off and pressed the hyperspace switch. The bus rocketed up and away only seconds before the planet exploded into a ball of fire.

Izzy glanced at the radar screen. The exploding planet was surrounded by a maze of lethal laser rays. They had to find a way through it to escape the blast . . . and quickly.

Can you find a way through the maze to safety?

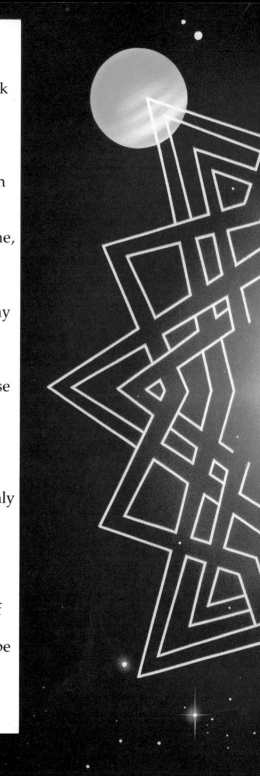

Back to Earth

And that was the last thing Tom and Izzy could remember. When they next opened their eyes, they were back in the High Street. They stumbled off the bus feeling very confused. Had their adventure really happened, or was it all a dream?

"Whatever happened to Roger and Norman?" asked Tom.

Izzy looked back at the bus and up and down the High Street. There was no sign of them anywhere. Or was there?

What do you think?

Clues

Pages 4-5

Hold the page in front of a mirror.

Pages 6-7

This is easy. Use your eyes.

Pages 8-9

Look carefully at each picture.

Pages 10-11

Where is the bus going? Where did Tom, Izzy and Roger get on?

Pages 12-13

Remember they are not from Nova.

Pages 14-15

Which is Roger's right in the photograph? Only one building matches Norman's description.

Pages 16-17

This is easy.

Pages 18-19

1=A, 26=Z. You will need to add punctuation marks.

Pages 20-21

Look at the other pictures of Tom.

Pages 22-23

You don't need a clue for this.

Pages 24-25

Which parts of the engine are broken? Are any parts missing?

Pages 26-27

The map is shown back to front. Use a mirror to read the instructions.

Pages 28-29

Which is the dashboard clock? To work out the speed of the bus, divide the distance it travelled by the time it took.

Pages 30-31

Join up the signal landmarks. What pattern do they make?

Pages 32-33

Piece the scraps together. The numbers don't increase by the same amount each time.

Pages 34-35

The Robots' message on page 19 tells you where to find Tom.

Pages 36-37

Look at the keys and the lock carefully.

Pages 38-39

The first defence disc goes here.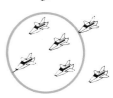

Pages 40-41

There are two entrances and exits.

Page 42

Keep your eyes and ears open.

Answers

Pages 4-5

The message is written back to front and upside down. To read it, turn the page the other way up and hold it in front of a mirror. This is what it says:

Who has dared challenge the Rogue Robots at their own game? Beware Earth-thing, soon you will be playing for your life. We shall strike when you least expect it.

Pages 6-7

Here you can see what Izzy spotted.

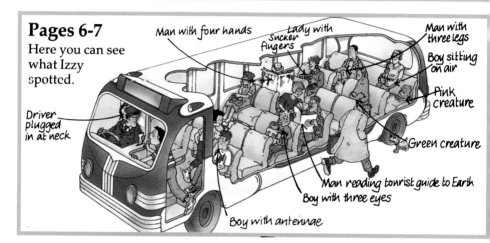

Man with four hands
Lady with Sucker fingers
Man with three legs
Boy sitting on air
Pink creature
Driver plugged in at neck
Green creature
Man reading tourist guide to Earth
Boy with three eyes
Boy with antennae

Pages 8-9

Here is the bus map.

Pages 10-11

The last stop, where Tom and Izzy boarded the bus, was Earth. Roger is travelling from Mars to Zenos and the bus is going to Juniper. The only line that stops at all these places is the Galactic Express. The next stop is Nova.

Pages 12-13

The only door they can all go through is the one labelled "Two-Eyed Aliens".

Pages 14-15

This is Norman.

He lives in this building.

Pages 16-17

Tom has been kidnapped. The pictures are numbered and arranged in the correct order to show exactly what happened to him.

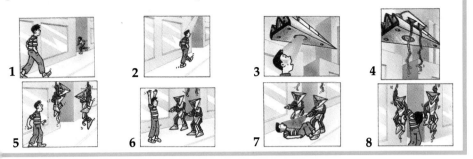

Pages 18-19

Each number stands for a letter, 1=A, 2=B and so on, while numbers are shown as small letters. You need to add punctuation marks for the decoded message to make sense.

Rogue Robot Ship to base on Robotica: Mission to kidnap Earth-thing successful. He will remain deep-frozen for 79 micro-minutes before being taken to the Challenge Chamber at 93:40. End of Message.

Pages 20-21

Izzy is right. There are several differences between the real Tom and this trick one.

Spot on wrong cheek

Wrong-shaped nose

Six fingers

T shirt with long sleeves and white collar

Pages 22-23

The kidnappers' vapour trail is shown in red.

45

Pages 24-25

All the broken or missing parts and their replacements are numbered in this picture.

To mend the bus, match the number of the broken or missing part with the spare of the same number.

Pages 26-27

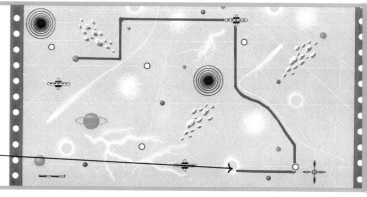

The route to Robotica is marked in red. Everything on the map is shown back to front.

The bus is here.

Pages 28-29

As the bus enters the skyway, the time is 93:15. The skyway signpost, the observation bulletin and the dashboard clock all show the same time.

It is 855 mega-miles to the Pluton exit. Here the patrolman stops the bus and the time on his watch reads 93:25. If this was correct, the bus would have travelled at 85.5 mega-miles per micro-minute, breaking the

speed limit for buses of 60 mega-miles per micro-minute.

The time on the dashboard clock is 93:30. It always shows the correct time, so the patrolman's watch must be wrong. This means that Roger drove 855 mega-miles in 15 micro-minutes at an average speed of 57 mega-miles per micro-minute. The bus was not breaking the speed limit.

Pages 30-31

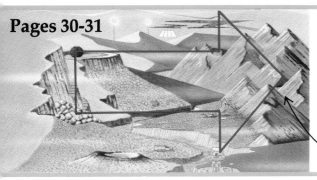

If lines are drawn joining the signal landmarks, they form an arrow pointing to the base.

The base is here.

Pages 32-33

This is the sequence with the missing numbers added. The jump between the numbers increases by two each time.

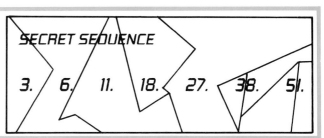

SECRET SEQUENCE

3. 6. 11. 18. 27. 38. 51.

Pages 34-35

Izzy, Roger and Norman are here. Their route to the map is marked in red. The message on page 19 says Tom will be taken to the Challenge Chamber. The only safe route is marked in black.

Pages 36-37

Try to imagine the other side of the keys. The pattern will be reversed.

Key number five is the only one that will open the door to the Challenge Chamber. It only matches the key shape if it is turned over, as shown here.

Pages 38-39

This picture shows how to isolate the enemy rockets with three defence discs, and so beat the computer.

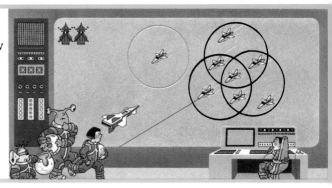

Pages 40-41

The route through the laser maze is shown in red.

Page 42

Several things, ringed in black, suggest that Norman and Roger are not far away.

First published in 1987 by
Usborne Publishing Ltd,
20 Garrick Street,
London WC2E 9BJ, England.

Copyright © 1987 Usborne Publishing Ltd

The name Usborne and the device 🐝 are Trade Marks of Usborne Publishing Ltd.